DK

What if...
EVERY VOLCANO ERUPTED AT ONCE?

Written by **EMMA YOUNG**

Illustrated by **SUPER FREAK**

CONTENTS

What if the sea wasn't salty?	4
What if meteorites never hit Earth?	6
What if the planet stopped turning?	8
What if Earth was upside down?	10
What if it was winter everywhere?	12
What if Earth's core turned to polystyrene?	14
What if the Sun switched off?	16
What if north pointed south?	18
What if you could walk everywhere on Earth?	20
What if we could predict earthquakes?	22
What if the Alps exploded?	24
What if every volcano erupted at once?	26
What if rocks were spongy?	28
What if we made buildings from rubies?	30
What if we knew next year's weather?	32
What if you could see the wind?	34
What if clouds were made of candy floss?	36
What if tornadoes didn't twist?	38

What if the sky was green?	40
What if you could touch a rainbow?	42
What if lightning went up?	44
What if you couldn't go surfing?	46
What if we drank all the water in the Amazon River?	48
What if the oceans were made of jelly?	50
What if all the ice melted?	52
What if every tree vanished overnight?	54
What if the planet's surface had no iron?	56
What if dead things didn't rot?	58
What if a rainforest swapped with a desert?	60
What if we could bring back extinct animals?	62
What if we had never invented plastic?	64
What if our maps were correct?	66
What if we couldn't see the stars at night?	68

Glossary/Index	70
Acknowledgements	72

What if the sea wasn't salty?

All the salt in the sea makes it easier for you to float around and swim in it. But if you get seawater in your eyes, it STINGS. And you certainly can't drink it. Why is the sea so salty? And wouldn't it be better if it wasn't?

One of the world's saltiest lakes is known as the Dead Sea. Almost nothing can live in it.

Heavy water

Every litre of seawater contains about 35 g (1 oz) of salt – that's about the weight of a chocolate bar. This makes the ocean VERY heavy...

SALT WATER

...If all the salt in seawater vanished, the sudden loss of weight could trigger earthquakes and volcanic eruptions! Also, the fresh water would kill most animals in the sea as they are adapted to live in salt water.

FRESH WATER

Space salt

Where did all this salt come from? Originally, it was in the dust and gas that collected together to form our planet, about 4.6 billion years ago. The building blocks of salt – sodium (an explosive metal) and chlorine (a poisonous gas) – were made in stars.

Clouds of hot, salty water erupt out of hydrothermal vents. The dissolved minerals in it can make the hot liquid look like smoke.

When the minerals in the hot liquid hit the cold seawater, they solidify, which creates a chimney that grows upwards.

Hydrothermal vent

Most of the salt in the ocean has been washed into it from the land. For millions of years, rivers and streams flowed over rocks containing salt, and it dissolved in that water and was then carried out to sea. Some sea salt, though, has come up from BELOW. Salt from underground rock can get spurted out of underwater volcanoes. It can also be spewed out in jets of hot liquid that burst from cracks in the ocean floor. These cracks are called "hydrothermal vents".

Many ocean fish that drink seawater have kidneys and gills that are BRILLIANT at getting rid of that salt.

The answer?

If the sea suddenly wasn't salty, we could drink it. BUT this would lead to earthquakes and volcanic eruptions. Not to mention a massive die-off of marine life. It would be a total disaster!

What if meteorites never hit Earth?

Meteorites are space rocks that have landed on Earth. Scientists love these rocks because they contain clues about the history of our planet. In fact, it seems that without meteorites, it would be VERY different. For a start, you wouldn't be reading this book!

Meteorite hunting

Antarctica is a great place to go meteorite hunting. That's because the dark rocks show up well against the snow and ice. Some of these meteorites have come from Mars or the Moon. But most were born in the "asteroid belt" – a ring of big rocks that lies between the orbits of Mars and Jupiter.

About **44 TONNES (49 TONS)** of meteoroids hit our atmosphere every day. That's around the weight of 44 cars.

The meteorite that wiped out the dinosaurs 66 million years ago was the size of a city.

Space rocks

An asteroid is a rock that orbits the Sun. A comet is a ball of dust and ice that orbits the Sun. Any bit that breaks off – or gets smashed off – an asteroid, a comet, a planet, or a moon is called a meteoroid. If a meteoroid comes flying towards Earth, and crashes into our atmosphere, it gets a new name: meteor. Most meteors are tiny and burn up, creating "shooting stars". But those that survive this fiery journey and reach the ground get rewarded with yet ANOTHER new name: meteorite.

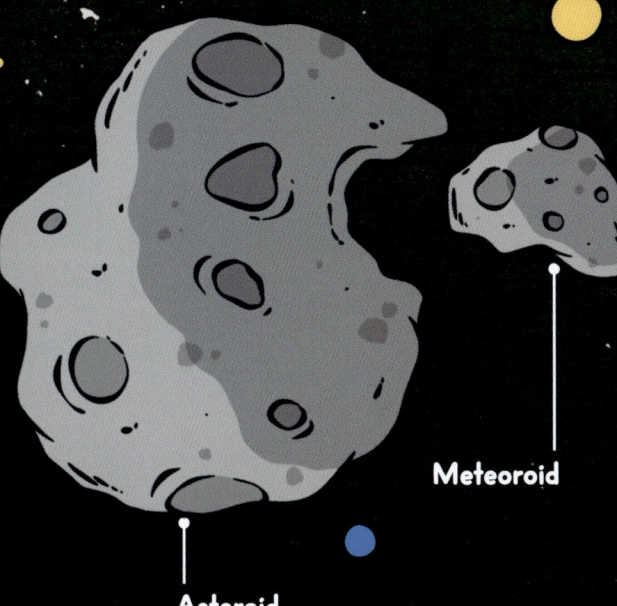

Meteoroid

Asteroid

Smashed and battered

Earth spent its first billion years being regularly battered by space rocks. Scientists think these meteorites were probably responsible for bringing the elements needed for life, as well as water, and all of the main building blocks of DNA – the instructions for how to make a body (including yours!).

The answer?

While they can cause damage, without meteorites, life may never have been able to get going on Earth. This means you probably have them to thank for your very existence!

7

What if the planet stopped turning?

Did you know that Earth is spinning at about 1,600 kph (1,000 mph)? You don't feel it because you, your home, the trees, the ocean, the air – everything, in fact – are spinning along with it, at the same speed.
But what if it stopped?

Sudden stop

If Earth suddenly stopped spinning, anything not anchored to the ground would keep on speeding along. That would include the seas, the atmosphere – and you. People would go flying. Trees would topple. Buildings would crumble. Massive tsunami waves would smash over the land. This would be bad!

Slow baked

Even if Earth stopped spinning gradually, we'd still be in trouble. Oceans would shift, putting most of North America, Asia, and Europe under water. When Earth stopped spinning completely, anyone left on the land would face days and nights that lasted for SIX MONTHS each. During those extremely long days, the Sun would bake the ground, and lakes and rivers would dry up.

During the six-month days, water would dry up in the heat.

Earth's spin is slowing down. When Tyrannosaurus rex was around, days were half an hour shorter.

Day to night

It takes Earth 24 hours to complete one complete spin, or rotation. When regions of the planet are facing away from the Sun, they're in darkness – it's night-time. When they're facing the Sun, it's daytime. Over 24 hours, people in any one place see dawn, then day, then dusk, then night. But not at the same time. For this reason, the globe is split into 24 "time zones". When it's 8.30am in London, UK, in December, it's 7.30pm in Sydney, Australia. If the planet stopped turning, the only change from day to night and back would happen as the Earth orbited the Sun, which takes a year!

London · New Delhi · Dakar · Sydney

During the six-month nights, it would be dark and cold.

The answer?

If Earth stopped turning, we'd all be in HUGE trouble. What kind of trouble would depend on how quickly it stopped, but once it had stopped still, not many plants and animals would be able to survive the six-month-long days and nights.

What if Earth was upside down?

Have you ever seen a map of the Earth? Then, you'll know that countries near the North Pole, such as Sweden, are shown towards the top, and those closer to the South Pole, such as Australia, are at the bottom. But what would happen if everything flipped upside down?

Summer swap

Did you know that when it's summer in the northern half of Earth (the "northern hemisphere"), it's winter in the south (the "southern hemisphere")? Assuming people survived the flip, those in the new "top" countries, like Australia and Chile, would have summer in July. People in the new "bottom" countries, like Sweden and the UK, would be out in December in sunglasses and shorts!

Sun switch

If the Earth was flipped, the Sun would rise in the new "west", instead of the east. And map apps would get very confused! That's because our system for locating any point on the planet is based on Earth being the "right" way up. Also, if you looked up at the night sky, you'd see a completely different pattern of stars.

Imaginary lines

Have you got any idea what "latitude 40.748817, longitude 73.985428" means? No? I don't blame you! In fact, it's a code for a specific place: the Empire State Building in New York City. Imaginary "lines of longitude" stretch between the North Pole and the South Pole, and go all the way around the planet. "Lines of latitude" circle the other way, around the equator, and up and down from there. Using these lines – and points in between them – we can give any spot on the planet its very own address. If the Earth flipped upside down, every point on the planet would get a new address.

There is no "top" or "bottom" in space.

The longitude "0" line goes through Greenwich, in London, UK.

The answer?

Seasons would swap. For many people, the Moon would suddenly look upside down. And, given their new locations, the climate of many countries would be totally transformed. A lot would change!

A glacier is a sheet of ice that's slowly moving under its own weight.

What if it was winter everywhere?

Have you heard of an "ice age"? It's a long cold period, when big areas of the planet are covered in thick sheets of ice. But what if the ENTIRE PLANET was covered in snow and ice?

Ice age

We are actually in an ice age right now — but only areas around the North and South poles are covered in ice. That's because we're enjoying a mild break from the super-cold. This break started about 10,000 years ago. Twenty thousand years ago, woolly mammoths and woolly rhinoceroses were roaming around, and it was far too icy for anyone to live in areas that are now fairly balmy.

Snowball Earth

Some scientists think that, in the past, our planet has been totally iced up. More than 635 million years ago, they think it froze over into a "hard snowball". Others think it might have been more like a "slush-ball" – but still very cold! Either way, some life managed to survive.

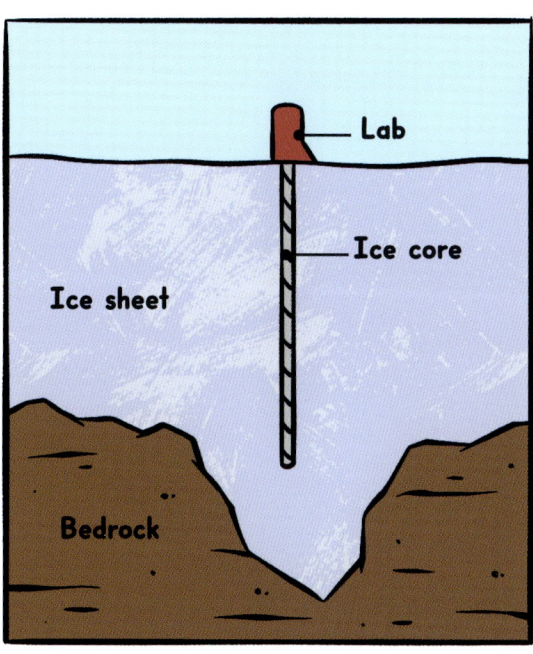

Ice cores

Ice cores are cylinders of ice that have been drilled out of an ice sheet or a glacier. These cores contain tiny bubbles of air that were trapped as the ice formed. The deeper the bubbles, the further back in time you go. By studying exactly what's inside them, scientists can look for changes in Earth's atmosphere. This work shows that levels of carbon dioxide – a "greenhouse gas" – have soared in the last 100 years, since we started burning lots of coal and other fossil fuels. Higher levels of these gases make the Earth warmer, so there is less snow and ice.

The answer?

At points in the past, it HAS been winter everywhere. We are in an ice age now, but scientists think the next really chilly bit will begin in 50,000 to 100,000 years' time. At this point, the ice sheets will spread. We won't get a total "snowball Earth", but life will get trickier for many animals and people.

There's a glacier in Greenland that's moving up to 40 m (130 ft) every day!

What if Earth's core turned to polystyrene?

What? Earth has a core? Yes – but it's not long like an apple core. It's a ball-shaped blob of metal. Polystyrene foam is often used to package electrical goods, like TVs. It's very light. Replace Earth's metal middle with THAT and some strange things would happen.

Crushed core

Polystyrene foam just couldn't support the weight of Earth. So, if the core was suddenly swapped, the planet would collapse in on itself, completely destroying the surface and everything on it!

Parts of the core are as hot as the surface of the Sun.

No more Moon

Earth's core takes up about an eighth of our planet, and it weighs A LOT - about 100 QUINTILLION TONNES (110 QUINTILLION TONS). A quintillion is a 1 with 18 zeroes after it! Swap that core with very light polystyrene, and the strength of Earth's gravity would become much weaker. That gravity is what keeps the Moon orbiting the Earth, and without it, the Moon would drift off into space!

Inside out

At the centre of our planet is the "inner core". This is a solid ball of mostly iron, plus a little nickel (a shiny metal). The huge weight of the Earth above it makes this iron solid. Around the solid inner core – where there is less pressure from above – is a river of liquid iron and nickel, called the "outer core". Above that is the "mantle" – a layer of hot, mostly solid rock. Finally, Earth has a skin, called the "crust". It's also made of rock, but it's cool and solid – which is a good job because you have to walk on it.

Earth's core is bigger than the planet Mercury.

The answer?

If Earth's metal core was replaced with polystyrene foam, the planet would implode! And we would lose the Moon.

What if the Sun switched off?

The Sun's rays can sometimes feel quite fierce. But that's nothing to what it's like up close! The Sun – our nearest star – is a massive power station that's churning out almost unbelievable amounts of energy. If it switched off, what would happen to us?

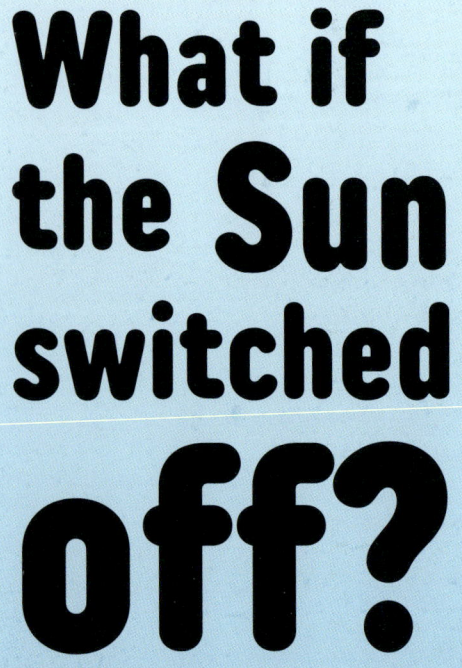

The Sun will **run out** of hydrogen fuel in about 5 billion years and **slowly die**.

Light and heat

The Sun's rays give us light and keep our planet warm. If it switched off, we'd be plunged into darkness. As plants need light to stay alive, they'd die. We'd also become extremely cold. The weather forecast everywhere would be: FREEZING!

Star power

You'd need about 44 MILLION big electric power plants to provide the energy that the Sun gives us every year. Almost ALL of the energy found on Earth came originally from our star. It's thanks to the Sun that flowers can grow, kangaroos can hop, and you have food to eat – and a body to eat it.

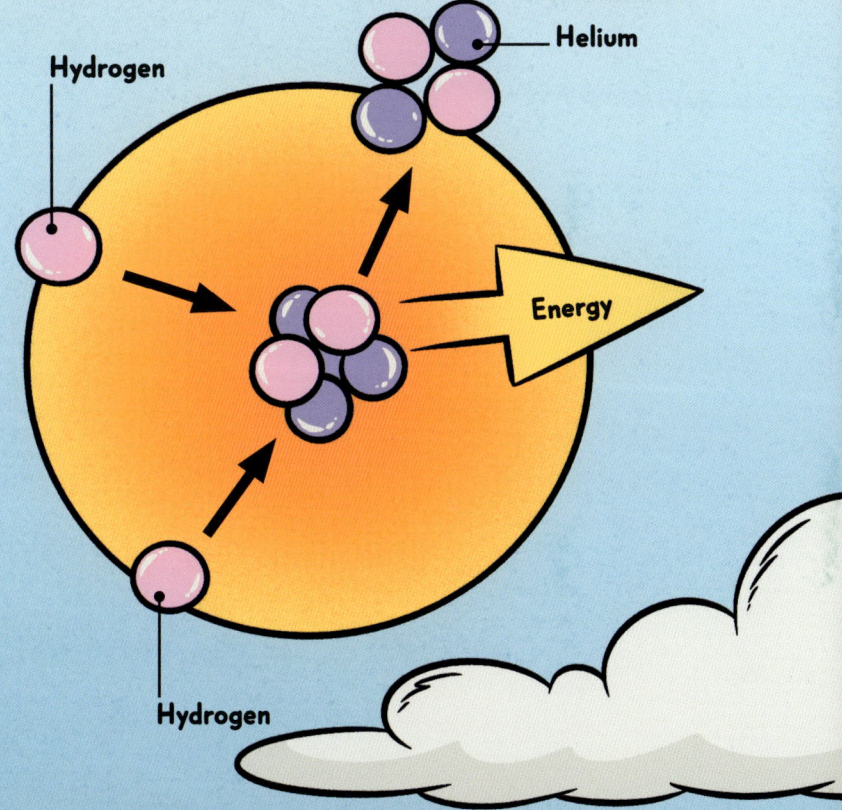

How the Sun works

The Sun is a massive ball of super-hot gas. Mostly, it's a gas called hydrogen. The temperature in the middle of the Sun is 15 MILLION °C (27 MILLION °F)! In this heat, the individual bits of hydrogen – the atoms – come apart, and the centres of them smash into each other, and join up. This process is called "fusion". The result is a new gas, called helium, and the unleashing of a MASSIVE amount of energy. This energy reaches us as heat and light.

Scientists are trying to find a way to use fusion to make energy on Earth.

The answer?

Without the heat and light from the Sun, we couldn't survive. Neither could most life on the planet. Eventually, even the oceans would freeze solid. Almost every living thing would starve or freeze. It's a good thing the Sun doesn't have a switch!

Giant magnet

Remember from page 15 how Earth's core holds liquid iron? This moving metal makes the planet into a giant magnet. Like every other magnet, Earth has two "poles": north and south. The poles are the two ends of a magnet where the magnetic force is strongest.

What if north pointed south?

Have you ever used a compass? If so, you'll know that they're marked "N" for North, "E" for East, "S" for South, and "W" for West. When the needle's pointing to "N", you know you're heading north. But why? And what if it flipped?

Invisible shield

Magnets have bubbles of magnetic energy around them. Earth's bubble – its magnetic field – is like an invisible shield. Harmful particles spewed out by the Sun bounce off it. At the North and South poles, though, these particles can get captured. This creates wavy, coloured ribbons in the sky – the northern and southern lights!

Some fish and birds, such as pigeons, use Earth's magnetic field to guide them.

Earth's magnetic field

The North Pole on a map is always in the same place. The same is true for the South Pole. BUT the two magnetic poles aren't in these exact locations. To make things EVEN MORE confusing, they can move! The "magnetic north pole" can move up to about 1,000 km (620 miles) away from the "map north pole"! Every so often, the magnetic poles do more than move — they flip, so that "N" becomes "S". While a flip is happening, Earth's magnetic shield weakens. This last happened about 780,000 years ago. If there was a flip today, harmful particles from the Sun could blast in and damage satellites, phone networks, and power supplies.

The first compasses were made in China more than 2,000 years ago.

The answer?

If north is pointing south, Earth's magnetic poles have flipped. Prepare for power cuts and satellite meltdowns!

What if you could walk everywhere on Earth?

Once upon a time, if humans had been around, they could have walked across all the land on the planet – without any annoying seas or oceans in the way. But the last time the land was joined together was about 200 MILLION years ago! So why isn't it like that today?

Sliding slabs

The top of Earth's rocky outer layers is made up of separate slabs, called tectonic plates. These slabs are packed pretty tight, but they're slowly moving on the hot, putty-like rock beneath.

The plates can push together, pull apart, or slide past each other. Where there are dips on the surface of these plates, water pools, forming seas and oceans.

One land

About 250 million years ago, Earth's slabs had moved in such a way that all the main chunks of land – the "continents" – had collided. They formed a single big blob of land, called Pangaea (said pan-JEE-a). This was the start of the Triassic Period – and DINOSAURS! About 200 million years ago, Pangaea started to break up.

Seven continents

Today, Earth's land is divided into seven continents. North America and South America are joined up. So are Africa, Asia, and Europe. Antarctica and large parts of Oceania are separated by water from the other continents. All of these continents also include many islands – even some giant ones, such as mainland Australia (Oceania) and Greenland (North America). Modern humans – like you – appeared only about 300,000 years ago, when Earth's land layout was basically as it is now. So no human could ever have walked everywhere on the planet.

The earliest dinosaurs could have walked over almost all of Earth's land.

The answer?

Because of where Earth's land is right now, you can't walk everywhere. But the plates are always slowly moving. If people are still around in millions of years, it might be possible then!

Sudden jolt

When there's a big earthquake, people usually feel a sudden jolt first. Then, the ground starts shaking. This can last for seconds or even minutes. Every year, on average, 10,000 people die in earthquakes, mostly because of buildings collapsing.

Tiny to HUGE

An earthquake's size is measured in "magnitude". People usually don't feel anything under about a magnitude 3. A magnitude 7 is a major earthquake. It can bring homes crashing down over a big area. A magnitude 9 can cause massive damage to buildings that are up to about 1,000 KM (620 MILES) apart.

What if we could predict earthquakes?

Every year, there are about 16 "major" earthquakes – quakes that are big enough to create serious damage. Right now, no one can predict them. But that doesn't mean scientists aren't trying...

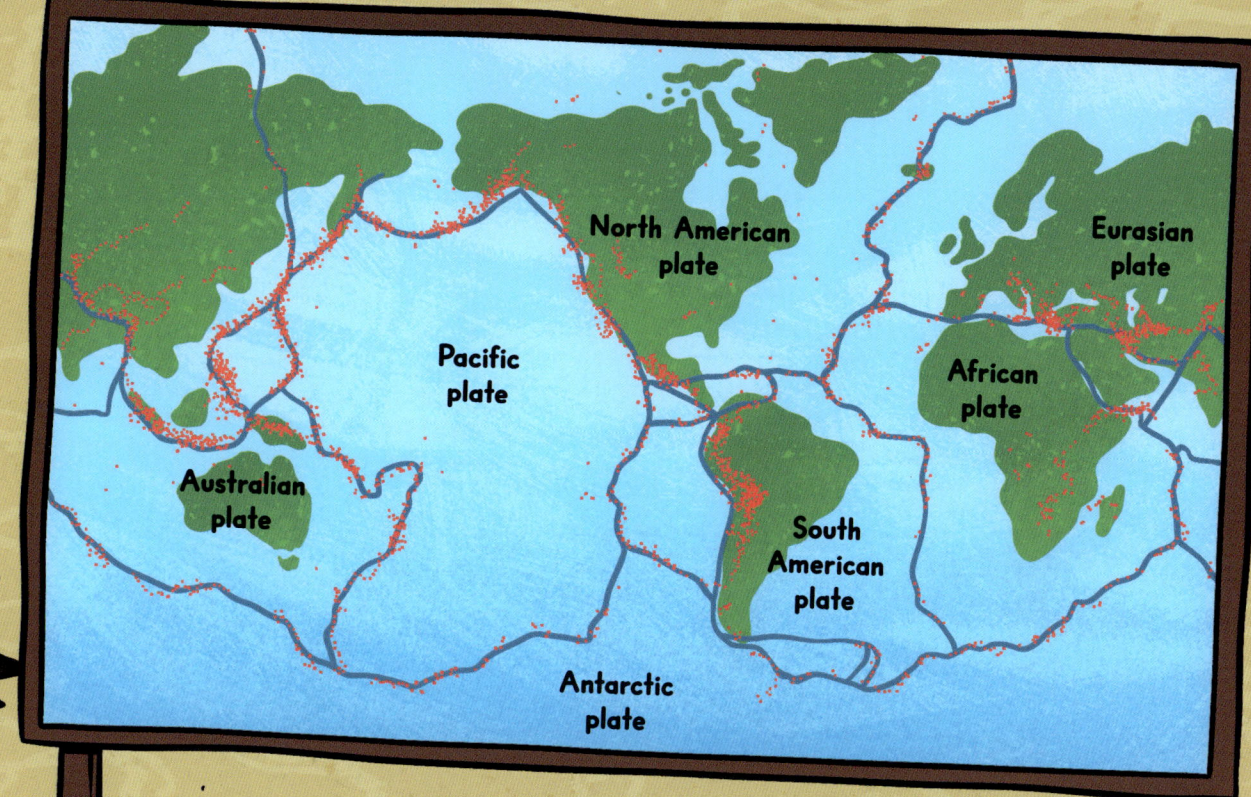

Where are earthquakes?

Do you remember from page 20 how Earth's surface is made up of tectonic plates? And that these plates are moving slowly on the hotter rock below? Where these plates grind past each other, they can catch. If they suddenly slip, energy is unleashed. This energy travels up through the ground – and there's an earthquake. The bigger the slip, the bigger the quake. Scientists think it might be possible to detect the first stages of a slip, about two hours before an earthquake actually happens. But right now, we don't have the technology to do this.

About 55 earthquakes (mostly tiny) happen every day.

The answer?

If we could predict major earthquakes even just two hours before they strike, alerts could get people to safety and save countless lives. Maybe you'll be the one to invent the kit to do it?

High peaks

The tallest mountain in the Alps – and in Europe – is Mont Blanc. It soars 4,809 m (15,778 ft) above sea level. That makes it about 50 TIMES taller than the Statue of Liberty in New York City – but it's just under HALF as high as the tallest mountain in the world, Qomolangma Feng (Mount Everest), which is 8,848 m (29,029 ft) tall.

Mauna Kea, a volcano in Hawaii, measures 10,000 M (32,800 FT) from its base to its peak – but about 6,000 m (19,700 ft) of it is under the ocean.

What if the Alps exploded?

The Alps? The mountain range that stretches about 1,200 km (750 miles) across EIGHT different European countries? If the whole lot exploded, obviously the people, animals, and plants that call the Alps home would suffer. But so would people living even thousands of miles away...

Water power

In the spring and summer, snow and ice on alpine mountains melts. This mountain water flows down the slopes and fills up important rivers. Some countries trap part of the flow in dams and use it to make electricity.

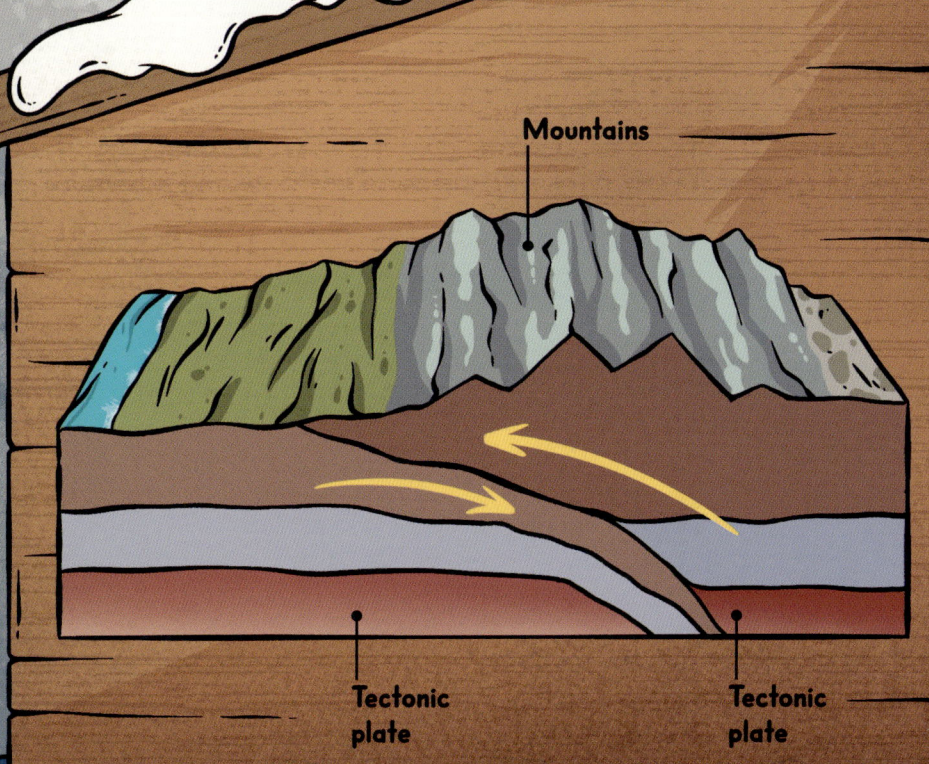

Making mountains

The Alps are just one of Earth's many incredible mountain ranges. In Asia, you'll find the huge Himalayas. The Andes runs along the entire west coast of South America. The Atlas Mountains in northern Africa separate the Sahara Desert from the Mediterranean Sea. And the Rocky Mountains stretch down the west of North America. These mountain ranges were all made by Earth's tectonic plates crashing into each other in slow motion. When rock at the edges of the plates crumpled, it was pushed up — into mountains.

It took tens of millions of years for the Alps to form.

The answer?

If the Alps exploded, Earth would lose one of its biggest mountain ranges. There'd be a massive loss of life, and rivers and power supplies across Europe would be changed for good. In a word: disaster.

What if every volcano erupted at once?

Volcanic bombs are lumps of hot rock that come hurtling out of a volcano.

Stinky sulphur

Volcanoes are little holes in Earth's outer layer, or "crust", from which hot, liquid rock can burst out. This liquid rock is called "magma" when it's below ground and "lava" as soon as it reaches the surface. Volcanoes also let out clouds of dust, ash, and gases, which can spread over thousands of kilometres. One of these gases is sulphur dioxide, which STINKS.

Every single year, around 50 to 70 volcanoes erupt. But Earth is home to more than 1,500 active volcanoes. Many of these haven't erupted in thousands of years – but could again. If they did all blow their tops at once, what would happen?

Mount Etna in Italy is almost always erupting.

Hot spots

"Active" volcanoes are ones that can still erupt. Most are found in the same places that most big earthquakes happen – where tectonic plates rub against each other. But you can also find odd volcanoes in "hot spots", where channels of magma reach right up through Earth's crust. The islands of Hawaii are a chain of volcanoes created by a hot spot.

Ash cloud
Lava
Magma
Crust
Magma chamber

Ready to pop

The hot layer beneath the Earth's crust is called the mantle. When a section of rock in the mantle melts, it becomes liquid magma, which is lighter than the harder rock around it. As more and more magma forms, it pushes against this rock, making it crack. The lighter magma then forces its way up through the crack – or cracks – and out as an eruption! When the magma cools, it hardens again. Most of Earth's surface was created by ancient volcanic eruptions. Fortunately, most of these ancient volcanoes don't contain magma any more, and will never erupt again.

The answer?

Spewing lava would cause problems for people living near volcanoes – but not just them. All the ash would form a thick cloud that would spread around the planet, blotting out the Sun. Also, gas from the eruptions would turn rain into ACID. In the end, most living things would be wiped out!

Hard rock

A "rock" is any solid collection of minerals. But rocks can be formed in different ways. Granite was made deep inside Earth. It's a hard rock. It is used for things like kitchen countertops because if you accidentally drop a glass on it, the glass will shatter – not the counter!

Even hard rocks can be broken up by weather over time.

What if rocks were spongy?

If I asked you for one fact about rocks, I bet you'd say: they're hard. If so, you'd be half-right! As far as scientists are concerned, while some rocks are "hard", others are "soft". And though there isn't a rock out there that you'd want to USE as a sponge, there are some that look like one!

Soft rock

Drop a stick of chalk and it'll smash into bits. Why? Because it's a "soft" rock. It's made up of tiny pieces of the shells of ancient sea creatures that have been squashed together over time to form a type of rock. But this rock is weak.

Making rocks

There are three main types of rock. The soft type, called "sedimentary rock", is made when grains of something – like bits of shell or sand – get squashed together over time. Then there's a type that's made when molten rock in or around volcanoes cools and hardens. This is called "igneous" (said IG-nee-uss) rock. This type of rock is hard. But the third type can be even harder. "Metamorphic" (said met-a-MOR-fik) rock is formed deep inside Earth, or where tectonic plates are crashing into each other. The different types of rock can change into each other by being melted or squashed – this is called the rock cycle.

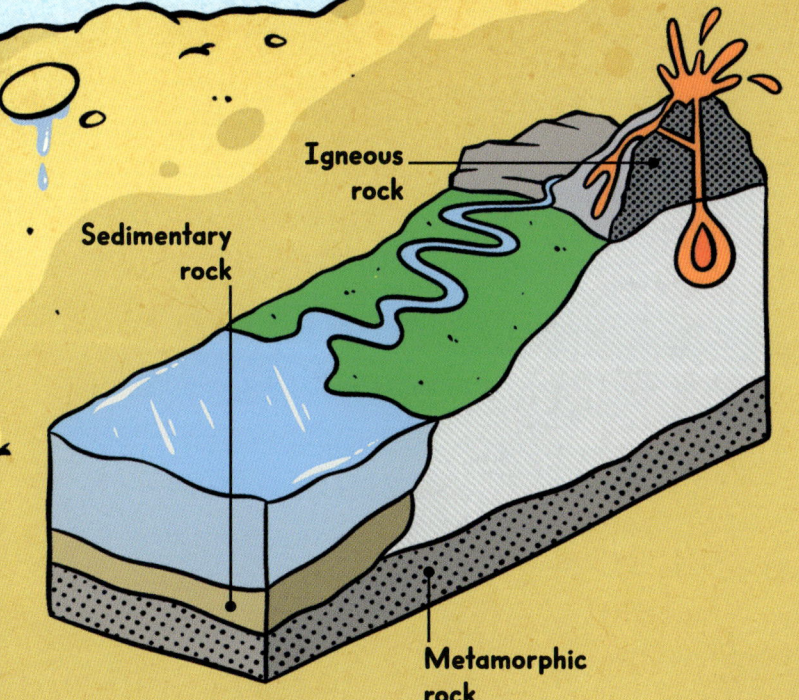

Sedimentary rock
Igneous rock
Metamorphic rock

Pumice is a rock that looks spongy because gas bubbles were trapped inside it as it was made.

The answer?

If rocks were spongy, the ground beneath your feet would squash down with every step. And it would be very tricky to construct buildings if the ground was squishy, especially with spongy stone! And mountains would sag down into the earth. It's a VERY good job they're not.

What if we made buildings from rubies?

Just imagine it: a city built not of dull grey concrete or bricks but sparkling red rubies! It would be amazing to look at. It would also be practically impossible. But why?

Red rubies

Rubies are glittering red crystals of a mineral with a dull name – "corundum" (said koh-RUN-dum). Sapphires, which are usually blue, are made of the same stuff. So, why are rubies red? It's because they also contain a tiny amount of a metal called chromium (said KROH-mee-um). The more chromium that's in there, the redder the ruby.

Cloudy rubies are more common than clear ones, and they're less valuable.

Dazzling insides

Earth's insides are home to all kinds of dazzling mineral gems. Along with rubies and sapphires, you can find diamonds (which can be colourless), green emeralds, purple amethysts, yellow citrines – and many more. But only a tiny fraction of Earth rock contains gems.

 Diamond    Ruby    Sapphire

 Emerald    Amethyst    Citrine

 +  +  +  =

Oxygen   Aluminium   Chromium   PRESSURE   Ruby

Earth made

All natural gemstones were created inside the planet. Diamonds are made of pure carbon (which is also the main ingredient in coal). They're what happens when carbon is squeezed REALLY HARD – as can happen deep underground. Rubies need monster pressure to form, too. When oxygen and aluminium (the metal kitchen foil is made from) get squished together, they turn into corundum. If there's also some chromium around, the result will be a ruby. BUT if there are also other metals in the mix, you won't get a red ruby, but a differently coloured stone. All of this means that sparkling red rubies are very rare.

Rubies can also be made in a lab.

The answer?

Those buildings would look spectacular! But rubies only form in very special conditions. This makes them rare – and expensive. If you wanted to make a building from blocks of ruby, it would have to be a small one. You'd also need LOTS of money!

Cow alert

The world's first weather forecast was for 31 July, 1861, for Great Britain and Ireland. Before that, people could only guess what the weather was going to be like. One popular idea was – and still is – that if cows are lying down in their fields, it's going to rain. But there's no evidence that this is true!

The hottest air temperature ever recorded was 56.7 °C (134.1 °F) in Death Valley, USA.

What if we knew next year's weather?

When's your next birthday? Wouldn't it be great to know exactly what the weather will be like on that day? Then, you could plan a celebration that would work for sunshine or rain – or maybe even a snow day!

All change

Scientists don't fully understand what makes our weather change. This makes it tricky to predict what the weather will be like in any one place next week, never mind next year. Forecasts for the next few days are usually right, though.

The wettest place on Earth is a village in India called Mawsynram. It gets around 10 times as much rain as New York City.

Cloud cover

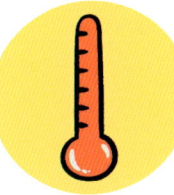
Temperature

Rain

Wind

Humidity

Pressure

What's the weather?

To know the weather in any one place on the planet, you have to know six different things. These are: how hot or cold it is (the temperature), how much cloud there is in the sky, how much rain is falling, how windy it is, how "humid" it is (how much water there is in the air), and also the "atmospheric pressure", which is the downwards weight of the atmosphere. To make a weather forecast you have to know how all these things are going to change. If you think that sounds pretty tough, you're right!

The answer?

It would be amazing to know what the weather will be like on any given day next year – you could plan what to wear in advance or when to go out and play games with your friends. But right now, not even supercomputers can tell us that.

What if you could see the wind?

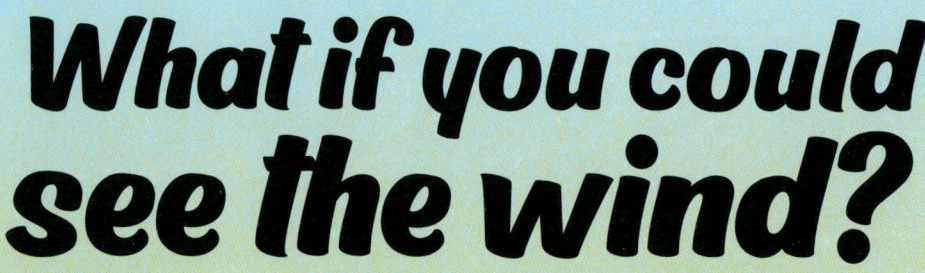

We all know what the wind FEELS like – sometimes soft and gentle, other times so strong, it can buffet us around! Wouldn't it be amazing to also SEE what's going on?

The fastest wind ever recorded on Earth was 407 kph (253 mph) in Australia in 1996.

Gentle wind

When a patch of air warms up, it becomes lighter – and rises. As this happens, cooler, heavier air sinks down to take its place. When these patches of air swap place slowly, they create a gentle wind. You'll feel it as a light, brushing tickle on your face.

Strong wind

If a warmer patch of air is A LOT lighter than the cooler, heavier air around it, they swap places quickly – and the wind will feel stronger. In summer, air over the oceans heats up and rises fast, but then it quickly cools and sinks, only to heat up again and rise. This fast switching can create a wind so strong, it gets the name "hurricane".

6
Light breeze
6 kph (4 mph)

38
Strong breeze
38 kph (24 mph)

62
Gale
62 kph (39 mph)

89
Storm
89 kph (55 mph)

118
Hurricane
118 kph (73 mph)

Types of wind

Scientists use a scale to tell us how strong the wind is blowing. When air is moving slowly, we feel a gentle wind, known as a "breeze". If the air is moving really fast, it's a "gale". A gale can break twigs off trees, but a "storm" wind can tear trees from the ground! The next big step up on the wind scale is a "hurricane". During a hurricane, wind is moving faster than 118 kph (73 mph). If you could SEE a hurricane wind, it would be travelling faster than a car on a motorway.

The answer?

You can't see wind because it's made of air, and air is invisible. But if you COULD see it, you'd see the air moving – sometimes even faster than a racing car. You could look out of the window and check if it was too windy to go out!

What if clouds were made of candy floss?

Clouds can certainly look like candy floss. So, what if they were actually made of the stuff – wouldn't that be brilliant? Well, it's a lovely idea... But it would mean the END of life as we know it!

Aeroplane trails are icy "cirrus" clouds made from water vapour from their exhaust.

Sky water

The clouds that look most like candy floss are called cumulus (said KYOO-myoo-luss) clouds. They are made up of droplets of water that are so tiny, they can stay up in the sky. It's only when they get bigger and heavier that Earth's gravity pulls them down towards the ground as rain.

Rain drain

This is a cumulonimbus cloud, also known as a thundercloud. These huge clouds drop rain, snow, or hail down onto our heads. They can be incredibly heavy. An average cumulonimbus weighs as much as a big passenger plane!

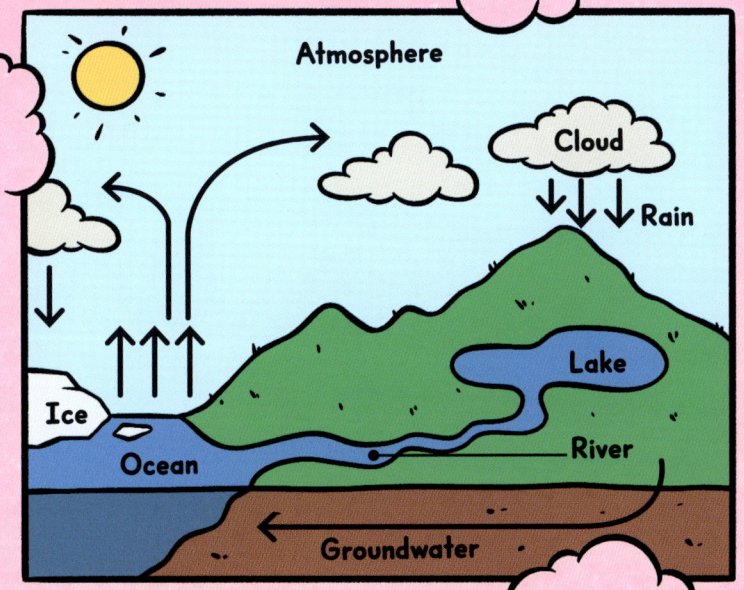

Water everywhere

When the Sun heats the Earth, water on land and in the ocean evaporates (it turns from a liquid to a gas). This "water vapour" rises. As it cools, it turns into little droplets of liquid water or solid ice crystals, and forms clouds. Eventually, this cloud water falls as rain, or – if it's cold enough – as snow. The process of liquid water becoming a gas that floats up, then turning into cloud, then falling as rain, then becoming a gas that floats up (and so on) is called the water cycle.

At any one time, about two-thirds of Earth is cloudy!

The answer?

If clouds were made of sugary candy floss instead of water, we'd have no rain. Rivers and lakes would shrink. The planet would dry up and no plants could grow. This would be very bad indeed!

A typical tornado moves across the ground at 16–32 kph (10–20 mph)

What if tornadoes didn't twist?

Do you know what a tornado's nickname is? It's "twister". That's because a tornado is a spinning column of wind. At the top, it touches a storm cloud. At the bottom, it grazes the ground. Another thing about twisters is, they can move ACROSS the ground much faster than you can run. That can make them very dangerous indeed.

Waterspouts are like tornadoes, but over the ocean.

Sky snatchers

The air in a tornado is rising FAST. This means that, like a vacuum cleaner, it can lift things up. Lighter things, including people, can be whisked up into the swirling wind. If the tornado's strong enough, cars – and even houses – can get tossed in the air.

How to make a tornado

For a tornado to occur, the conditions have to be right. First, there has to be a massive thunderstorm. Inside a thundercloud, warm air rises. If there are strong winds around a thundercloud, the rising warm air can start to spin. This spinning wind can drop vertically from the cloud. When it touches the ground, it gets the name "tornado". Tornadoes can spin for hours, but usually only last several minutes.

Seeing air

How can you see a tornado if it's made of wind – which as you know from page 34, we can't normally see? It's because tornadoes are often filled with water droplets and dust – not to mention bigger things they've picked up, such as pebbles or cars! We see all these things spinning in the wind.

The answer?

If a tornado didn't twist, it wouldn't be a tornado! The wind wouldn't be able to pick up cars and houses, and chuck them around in the same way, which would prevent a lot of damage.

39

Blue sky

Sunlight is made up of "waves" that are all the colours of the rainbow. When sunlight hits the gases in the atmosphere, the blue waves and green waves in it get scattered around, including down towards us. This affects what we see when we look up. But because our eyes are more sensitive to blue light than green light, the sky looks blue, rather than blue-green.

What if the sky was green?

On a clear day, the sky is blue. Unless the Sun is rising or setting, in which case, it might be pink or peach – or even orange or red! The sky can be quite a lot of colours. But not green. If it DID turn green, you should be worried...

Great atmosphere

Earth's atmosphere is a blanket of air that reaches all the way from the ground to about 10,000 km (6,200 miles) above your head. It's made up of a mix of gases as well as clouds and some tiny grains of solids, such as dust and soot.

In the middle of the day, the Sun is overhead and light has a short distance to travel.

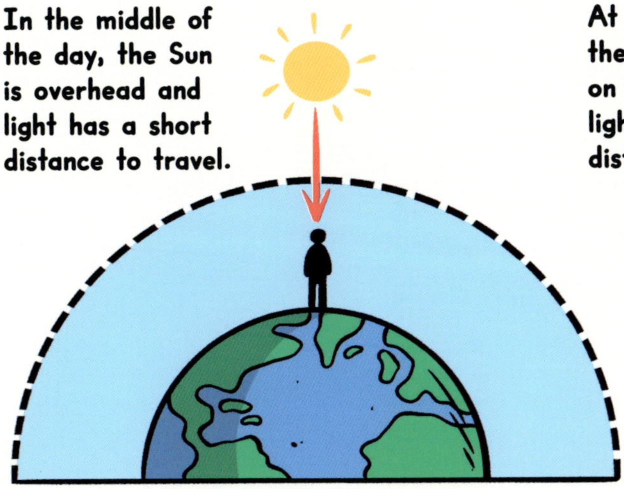

At dawn and dusk, the Sun is low on the horizon and light has a longer distance to travel.

If we had no atmosphere, the sky would be black!

Midday

Sunrise and sunset

Dawn to dusk

Our air is mostly a gas called nitrogen, plus some oxygen, and small amounts of other gases. Nitrogen and oxygen scatter blue light waves more than the other colours. At sunrise and sunset, light from the Sun has to travel through more of Earth's atmosphere to reach us than at midday. During this longer journey, blue light gets so scattered that it's mostly gone from the light that reaches our eyes. This happens to green waves, too. What's left? Yellow, orange and red light – which is what we often see at dawn and dusk.

Lots of smoke in the air can make the Sun and the Moon look bright red.

The answer?

If the sky suddenly turned green, one of two things has happened. Either the air has changed, or your eyes have changed. Both would be a surprise!

41

The Vikings believed that a rainbow bridge connected Earth to the world of the gods.

What if you could touch a rainbow?

It has just been raining, and the Sun is coming out and – WOW – now there's an incredible rainbow arcing through the sky! Those colours can look so brilliantly bright and vivid. Wouldn't it be fantastic to reach out and touch them?

Full circle rainbow

When we're on the ground, we see rainbows as curves through the sky. But if you were standing on top of a tall building, or flying in an aeroplane, you might be lucky enough to see a FULL CIRCLE rainbow below you!

Moonbows

It is possible to see rainbows at night. These "moonbows" happen when: 1) It's raining and 2) Sunlight that has bounced off the Moon hits the rain. Because light that comes to us from the Moon is much weaker than light straight from the Sun, moonbows are much fainter than rainbows.

Sunlight

The different waves of light can be seen as different colours.

The curved surface of the raindrop splits the sunlight.

What rainbow?

Sunlight is made up of different "waves" of light. When they are all mixed together, the light looks white to us. But when these waves are separated out, we see them as having their own unique colour. When light from the Sun hits big, round drops of rain, the waves are separated out – and we see all those colours. They always appear in the same order: red, orange, yellow, green, blue, indigo, and violet. If you move towards a rainbow, though, it will appear to move too. That's because you only see it when you're in the right place in relation to the raindrops. You'll never be able to touch it because it's made of light.

Red rainbows can appear at sunrise or sunset when the Sun is low in the sky.

The answer?

Sadly, you can't touch a rainbow because it isn't a solid object! If you want a rainbow you can touch, you'll have to paint one.

43

What if lightning went up?

Have you ever seen lightning? There's a good chance you have because it flashes somewhere in the world THREE MILLION times a day! Though we often think of lightning as starting in the sky and zapping downwards, in fact, it can do some very strange things...

About a quarter of a million people are hit by lightning bolts every year.

Lightning is five times hotter than the surface of the sun.

Two types

Lightning is a massive spark of electricity. It comes in two main types. There's "forked" lightning, which is the lightning bolt type that strikes the ground. And there's "sheet" lightning, which stays inside clouds and lights them up.

Strange strikes

Lightning usually starts in a storm cloud. Less often, a helicopter flying close to a storm cloud can trigger a lightning strike, as can an erupting volcano, and even heavy snow! When lightning sparks, it makes a huge noise. But because the light flash reaches you faster than the sound waves, there's a gap before you hear the sound as thunder.

Up and down

The winds in storm clouds can be very strong. These gusts tumble water droplets and hail around inside the cloud, which can create a build-up of electric charge. When that charge gets strong enough... ZAP! There's a spark of electricity, which we call lightning. This lightning might stay inside the cloud or travel between clouds – or jump to the ground. Lightning can, in fact, go upwards, too. But this only really happens in high places – like the top of a mountain or a skyscraper – and only when they have just been hit by a downwards bolt from a storm cloud.

Cloud to cloud lightning
Lightning trapped in cloud
Cloud to air lightning
Cloud to ground lightning

The answer?

Lightning CAN go up – but it doesn't happen often. To have a chance of seeing it, you'll have to be looking up at the tip of a skyscraper or a mountaintop during a thunderstorm. Just make sure that you're safe somewhere inside!

45

What if you couldn't go surfing?

I mean, EVER. What if you couldn't go surfing, or bodyboarding, or even jump a wave at the beach because there weren't any waves anywhere on the planet? Well, if this happened, it would be a DISASTER! And not just for surfers...

Stormy start

Wind makes waves. The stronger the winds, the bigger the waves. If you've ever seen massive waves crashing on a beach, they probably began life in a storm out in the ocean. They might have travelled thousands of miles before hitting the shore!

High and low

When a tide is "high", the sea comes right up on a beach, knocking down sandcastles or swamping deckchairs. When it's "low", you might have to walk for a long time over wet sand to reach the water. The tides are created not by wind, but the movement of the Moon around our planet.

Breaking waves

If you've ever been out at sea on a boat, you might have seen big waves rolling through the water. (You might have felt them, too!). But why does a rolling wave "break" or "crash" when it gets close to a beach? This is because as the seabed gets shallower, it starts to drag on the bottom of the wave, slowing this part down. But the top part of the wave – the "crest" – keeps rolling on. This causes the crest to curl over, and then collapse into frothing surf.

Wave crest — **Beach** — **Seabed drags on the bottom of the wave**

The HIGHEST wave ever surfed was just under 30 M (98 FT) tall!

The answer?

If no one can go surfing or even wave-jumping because there are no more waves, this is BAD because it means there's no wind. And if there's no wind, something has gone VERY badly wrong with Earth's air!

What if we drank all the water in the Amazon River?

Well, that would take us a bit of time! The Amazon River, in South America, is famous for being massive (as well as being home to flesh-eating piranhas!). It carries more water than any other river in the world. So what WOULD happen if we drank it dry?

Piranhas have fearsome teeth, but they usually only eat other fish.

Wet and wetter

The Amazon starts high in the Andes Mountains, in Peru, and empties into the Atlantic Ocean. During the dry season, it can be about 4-5 km (2-3 miles) wide. In the wet season, when there's a lot more rain, it can expand to a width of 50 KM (31 MILES) and rush along about as fast as you can jog.

Dry death

If the Amazon dried up, all the fish and other river creatures that live in it would die (including the piranhas, and also pink river dolphins). But so would trees and animals throughout the Amazon Rainforest. They depend on water from both the Amazon River itself, as well as more than a thousand smaller rivers that branch off it.

The world's longest river

The Amazon River carries more water than any other river, but it isn't the longest. That world record goes to the Nile, which snakes its way up through northeastern Africa before emptying into the Mediterranean Sea. The Amazon comes second, and after that is the Yangtze River in China (home to the very rare Chinese alligator). Then comes the Mississippi, which passes through no fewer than TEN US states. The fifth longest river in the world, the Yenisey, in Asia, gets so cold in winter, it freezes over. Many people depend on these huge rivers for water.

Length of river:
- Nile: 6,695 km (4,160 miles)
- Amazon: 6,400 km (3,977 miles)
- Yangtze: 6,300 km (3,915 miles)
- Mississippi: 5,971 km (3,710 miles)
- Yenisey: 5,539 km (3,442 miles)

The Amazon is **a milky brown colour** because it carries **mud** down from the **Andes Mountains**.

The answer?

Not only would it be a huge task to drink that much water, but if the Amazon River ran dry, the whole of northern South America would suffer. The Amazon Rainforest is filled with unique plants and animals that wouldn't survive without the water from the river. Let's not do it!

> The world's deepest place is the Mariana Trench. It reaches 11 KM (7 MILES) below the surface of the Pacific Ocean.

What if the oceans were made of jelly?

Well, for one thing, you could walk EVERYWHERE on Earth! For another, when you got peckish, you could nip down to the beach for a tasty mouthful. But if you're thinking that maybe there would be downsides too, you'd be right!

Sea or ocean?

There isn't actually much of a difference between seas and oceans. It's just that oceans are massive, and seas are smaller and usually partly surrounded by land. In fact, many seas are part of bigger oceans. Take the North Sea. It's part of the Atlantic Ocean, but has land on three sides – a seal swimming in the North Sea is also swimming in the Atlantic Ocean.

One ocean

We give five of the biggest oceans their own names: the Pacific Ocean, the Atlantic Ocean, the Indian Ocean, the Arctic Ocean, and the Southern Ocean. The Pacific is the largest. It covers just under a third of Earth's surface! But, if you look at a globe or a world map, you'll see that the oceans are all connected. This one united ocean is called the "Global Ocean". Oceans are basically massive puddles of water that have pooled in the dips in Earth's crust. These mega-puddles are so full, they have joined up — so a fish could swim between all of them.

Anglerfish and algae

The ocean is home to some strange-looking creatures, such as the sea pig and the anglerfish — which has massive spiky teeth. It's also home to a surprising amount of microscopic, plant-like algae, which don't look as exciting, but which have a VITAL job — they make about half of the oxygen on Earth.

Most of Earth's surface — **71 per cent** — is covered in ocean.

The answer?

If the oceans turned to jelly, everything in them would die. Without doubt, it would be the worst jelly disaster ever!

Ice worms live in glacier ice in North America. They eat algae in the snow!

Squashed snow

Glaciers are basically snow that has been squashed for a long time under its own weight into ice. They're found in the coldest regions of our planet. Icebergs are bits of a glacier that have broken off and floated free.

What if all the ice melted?

Have you ever watched an ice cube in a drink? Icebergs are basically the same – but bigger. Still, they're nowhere near as big as the VAST chunks of ice that they broke off from. In fact, about two thirds of all the fresh water on Earth is frozen solid in ice. And if all that ice melted… What do you think might happen?

Cold sheets

Ice sheets are MASSIVE glaciers. Right now, Earth has two. One covers most of Greenland, the other blankets, or "sheets", Antarctica. The Antarctic ice sheet is the biggest single chunk of ice on Earth.

Total melt

If the Antarctic ice sheet WAS an ice cube, you'd need a glass at least 5 KM (3 MILES) deep and the size of the USA and Mexico combined! Areas where it extends over the ocean are known as "ice shelves". Icebergs regularly break off these ice shelves. When big chunks of a glacier come away and fall into the sea, or when icebergs melt, the level of the sea against the land (the sea level) goes up. Scientists think that if ALL the ice on Earth melted, sea levels would go up by 70 m (230 ft).

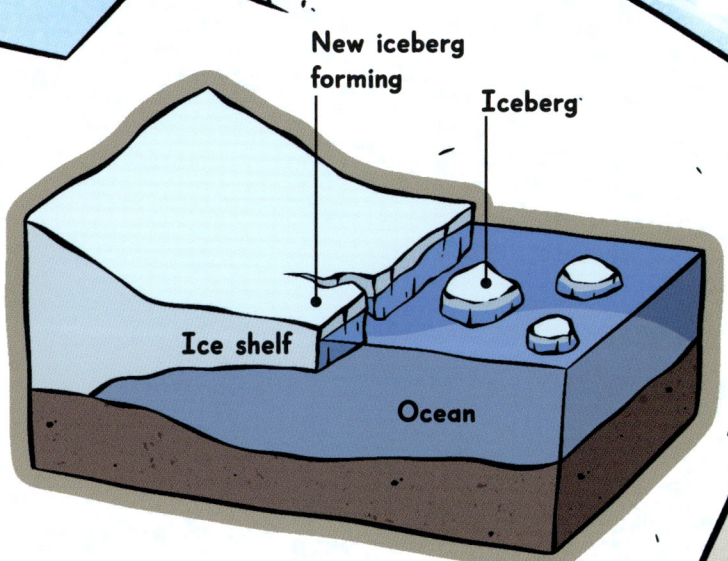

The answer?

If all the ice on Earth melted, sea levels would shoot up. This would mean that low-lying countries would get submerged. All of the Netherlands and Bangladesh, as well as most of Denmark, would be underwater, and so would many other places. Lots of people would lose their homes. This would be a disaster!

What if every tree vanished overnight?

Every. Single. Tree. From the towering California redwoods of America's Pacific coast to Yemen's dragon blood trees! (These trees get their name because they ooze a sticky red sap!). It's hard to imagine a world without trees. But actually living without them would be FAR harder...

The world's tallest tree is 116 m (381 ft) high and the world's oldest tree is 5,000 years old.

Trees in numbers

There are about 3 TRILLION trees in the world. That's about 400 for every person. The biggest forest anywhere is in Russia. It's home to more than a fifth of the world's trees and it's bigger than any country – apart from Russia!

Forest bath

"Forest bathing" means spending peaceful time among trees. You might hug a tree, listen to the sound of birds singing, or focus on the smells of the forest. In Japan, forest bathing is part of the national health programme. It helps people to relax and feel better.

Tree power

Trees have a LONG list of crucial jobs. They provide a home to animals, and some other plants. They clean the air by trapping harmful chemicals. They suck water up out of the ground and pump it into the air, helping clouds to form. They help to cool the air. They hold soil in place, so it doesn't get washed away by rain. They also mainly breathe in the opposite way to us – taking in carbon dioxide and releasing oxygen as waste. And much more!

- Habitat
- Clean air
- Make clouds
- Cool air
- Fix soil
- Make oxygen

The answer?

Firstly, we wouldn't be able to make anything out of wood, from pencils to boats. But much worse, the vital jobs that trees do wouldn't get done. So, rain would lead to terrible flooding, Earth would get hotter, and all the extra carbon dioxide would poison the air and turn the seas to acid!

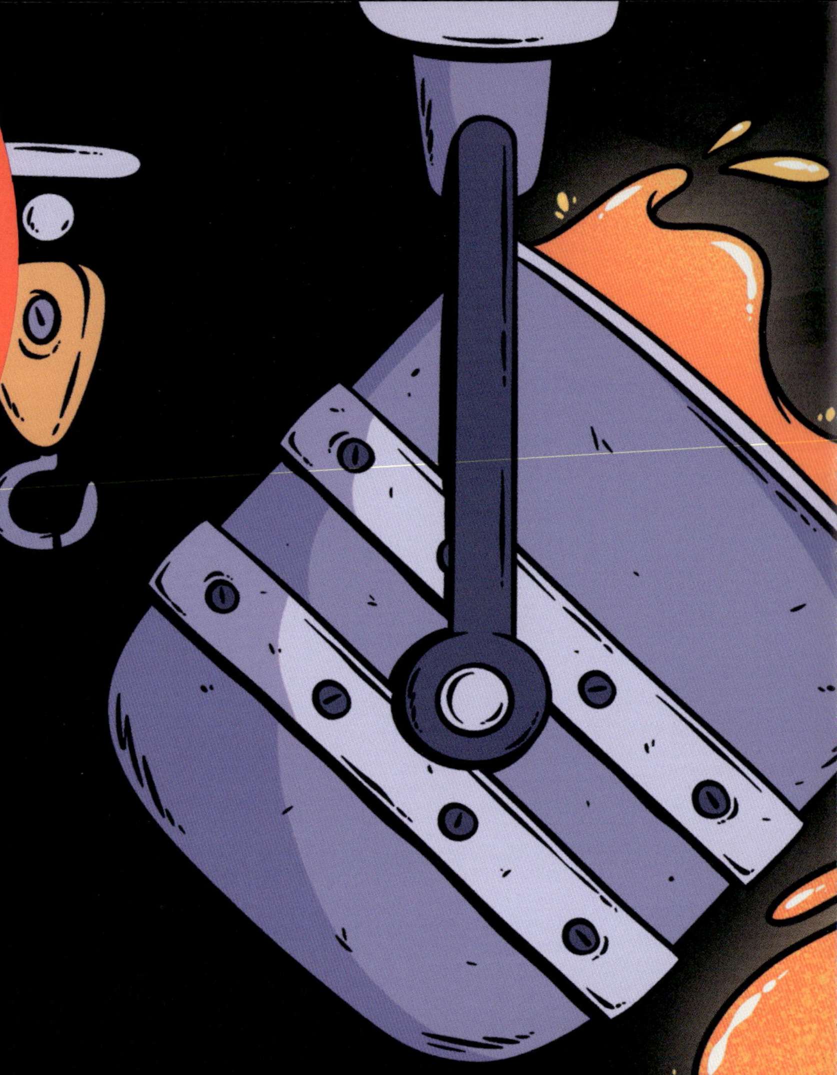

Bodies and bridges

Steel is about 99 per cent iron. We use steel to make the strong skeletons of everything from bridges to football stadiums. Even you are about 0.01 per cent iron. Your red blood cells use iron to grab oxygen from the air to keep your cells alive (iron also makes them red, but that's another story)!

What if the planet's surface had no iron?

If you've read page 14, then you know what would happen if the iron in Earth's core disappeared (it's not good news!). But would it really make much difference if Earth's surface didn't have any? The answer is YES!

Mars looks red because it's covered in rusted iron.

Precious metals

Iron is a very important "resource". A resource is any natural thing that people use and value. Water is a resource, as is wood from trees, or even cocoa beans (without cocoa beans, there'd be no chocolate). Many metals are valuable resources – such as cadmium used in batteries, aluminium used in aeroplanes, and iron for steel.

Making steel

To make steel, first we have to dig iron out of the ground. But it doesn't come out as pure iron. Rather, it's packaged up with its best friend – oxygen. Together, iron and oxygen make "iron ore". If you put chunks of iron ore with a few other ingredients in a big hot oven (called a blast furnace), the oxygen gets stripped away, and molten iron pours out at the bottom. Iron by itself is not especially strong. But if you then add a little bit of carbon (from coal), it becomes strong steel!

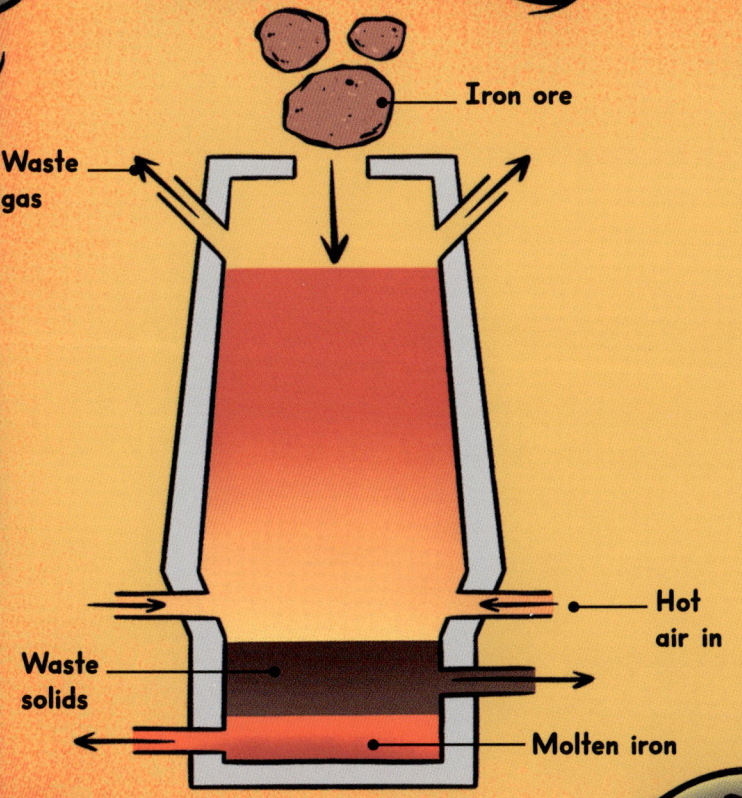

The answer?

Without iron, there would be no steel for buildings, and you might be wondering where your TV and fridge had gone. Except you wouldn't, because without iron, there'd be no you!

We dig more than 2 TRILLION TONNES (2.2 TRILLION TONS) of iron ore out of the ground each year.

Vital rot

Cells are built from different substances, such as carbon, proteins, and water. When a living thing dies, its cells start to break down or "rot", releasing these substances back into the soil, where they can be used by plants to grow. Bacteria and fungi have an important role in this process – they feed on dead cells, which helps the cells to break down more quickly.

> Burning Fossil Fuels releases carbon dioxide - a "greenhouse gas".

What if dead things didn't rot?

Eew. Just imagine if every living thing, from trees and insects to slugs and birds, didn't rot when it died. Yes, the planet would be covered in mounds of dead things. Although, not all dead things rot away completely, and if they did our lives would be different, too.

Rotting food is bad for you because bacteria that love to eat dead cells make nasty toxins.

Buried energy

Have you heard the term "fossil fuel"? It's used for fuels that we get out of the ground and burn for energy, including coal, natural gas, and oil. The reason for the name is simple – these fuels are made from the fossilized remains of dead things! But importantly, these particular dead things didn't TOTALLY rot away before they were transformed into fuels.

Dead plants fall into a swamp and don't rot completely.

The plants are squashed over millions of years.

Eventually, the plant remains become coal.

Fossilized Fuels

Fossil fuels take MILLIONS of years to form. Coal was made when lots of dead plants were squished in a swamp, buried by mud, and left for AGES. Oil and natural gas were made when minute sea life fell to the bottom of the ocean, were buried by mud, and then left for AGES. Instead of rotting away completely, the buried remains were transformed into fossil fuels, trapping the energy stored inside them when they were alive. When fossil fuels are burned, that energy is released as heat and light!

The answer?

If dead things didn't rot, dead plants and animals would be left everywhere! Scavengers, such as vultures, would be happy with all that extra food, but nutrients would slowly be sucked out of the soil and never returned. Without rot, plants and animals would gradually die out.

Hot and wet

Plants and animals in the Amazon Rainforest evolved in hot, wet conditions. Many trees have waxy leaves with pointed tips, to help water to run off them. The toucan's enormous bill helps it to get rid of body heat.

Nutrients in dust that's blown from the Sahara help to feed the Amazon Rainforest.

What if a rainforest swapped with a desert?

Let's say the Amazon Rainforest, in South America, swapped places with the Sahara Desert, in northern Africa. The Amazon Rainforest is a vibrant, wet jungle, packed with all kinds of life. The Sahara is Earth's biggest hot desert. If you're thinking, "This could be interesting", you'd be right!

Deserts don't have to be hot. Antarctica is Earth's biggest desert.

Hot and dry

There isn't enough rain in the scorching Sahara to support lots of life – and so there isn't much food for animals. Dromedary camels have a brilliant solution: they store energy, in the form of fat, in their hump. A hump can hold about the weight of an 11-year-old in fat! Bactrian camels use the same trick, but they have two humps.

Different biomes

Regions of the planet that have a similar climate are called biomes. Hot desert is a type of biome. So is rainforest. (As are cold desert, cold forest, temperate (mild) grassland, temperate forest, and tropical grassland). The Sahara Desert and the Amazon Rainforest are both close to the equator. This makes them hotter than areas that are further north or south. About 6,000 years ago, the Sahara region also got lots of rain, and was covered in grassland. But then the world's weather patterns shifted and this part of Africa became very dry. If the Sahara and the Amazon swapped places, they'd have a totally different climate.

The answer?

If the Amazon Rainforest was plonked where the Sahara Desert is now, it would still be hot – but it would become VERY dry, and would gradually turn to desert. The Sahara Desert, in its new location, would become green. So, you'd have the Amazon Desert and the Sahara Rainforest! New species of plants and animals would appear in each place over time.

61

What if we could bring back extinct animals?

When an animal goes extinct, that means there are none left anywhere in the world. At least, none that are alive... So, what if we could bring some of these creatures back? What would you most like to see running around again? A woolly mammoth? A sabre-toothed tiger? What about a T. rex?

Human effects

99.9 per cent of species that were alive on Earth at one point in time have gone extinct. In the past, natural events caused most of these losses. But right now, humans are having a big impact. Clearing land to produce food for us is one of the biggest threats to wildlife.

De-extinction

Scientists call reversing extinction "de-extinction". Some people hope to make the dodo (a flightless bird from the island of Mauritius) de-extinct. They say this could help bird conservation. Others think that instead, we should be focussing on stopping the damage we're doing to our environment now to prevent any more species going extinct.

 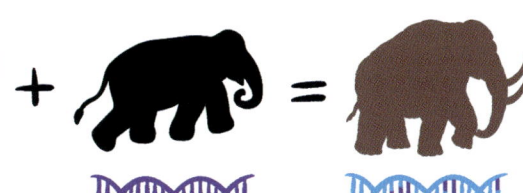

Return of the mammoth

To make an organism de-extinct, you need its DNA. This contains the instructions on how to build its body. In the right conditions, DNA can be found inside cells that have been dead for a very long time. In fact, scientists have been able to get well-preserved DNA from a woolly mammoth that died more than 50,000 years ago! Now, they're working on tweaking the DNA inside cells from the closely related Asian elephant to match this woolly mammoth DNA. The next step is to try to grow these cells into animals that are VERY SIMILAR to woolly mammoths, though they won't be exactly the same.

Woolly mammoths went extinct after the Great Pyramid of Giza was built.

DNA from a million-year-old mammoth has been extracted from its tooth.

The answer?

Scientists already have plans to bring back extinct animals – or, at least to create animals that are very similar to ones that have died out. It would be amazing to see real life dinosaurs – but they would need somewhere to live, and something to eat!

Plastic pollution

You can find plastic in everything from toothbrushes and clothes to furniture and toys. One quarter of all plastic that we use is in packaging for food and other things that we buy. A lot of this plastic isn't recycled, but ends up polluting soils and oceans.

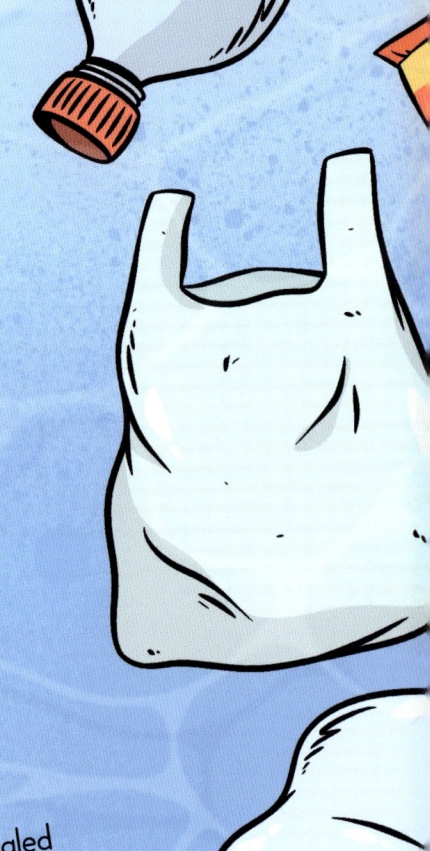

What if we had never invented plastic?

Modern plastic was invented in 1907. Suddenly, we had a material that was light, strong, cheap, and didn't rot. Brilliant! Except that because it's light, strong, and cheap we make about 400 MILLION TONNES (440 MILLION TONS) of it every year. And because plastic takes CENTURIES to rot, that waste is causing MASSIVE problems.

Water waste

Bigger bits of plastic can get tangled around sea creatures, including birds, turtles, and fish. Smaller bits can look like tasty food — and clog up animals' stomachs. Eventually, the plastic breaks down into very small pieces. But these tiny fragments still make wildlife sick.

Ocean garbage patch

Because a lot of plastic rubbish is light, it gets washed into rivers and from there it floats to the ocean. In some places, swirling ocean currents trap vast amounts of it. In an area known as the Great Pacific Garbage Patch in the Pacific Ocean, there are thought to be 1.8 TRILLION pieces of plastic. Some people are trying to remove this plastic, but the best thing is to stop it ending up there in the first place. Everyone can make a difference by always putting rubbish in the bin and recycling plastic where possible.

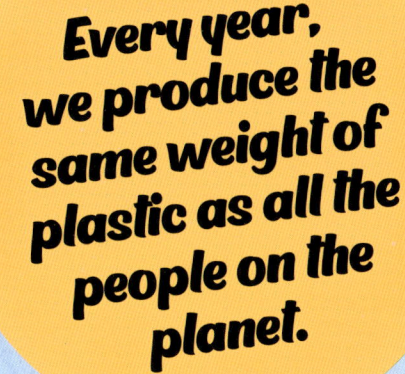

Every year, we produce the same weight of plastic as all the people on the planet.

When a plastic object is recycled, it's melted and formed into something else.

The answer?

Plastic has a huge impact on the world. There are upsides – for example, it's a cheap way of insulating electrical wires. Without plastic, you might not have electric lights in your home. But without plastic there would be much less pollution in Earth's soils and oceans. Plastic has changed things for better and for worse, and our lives would be very different without it!

I'm smaller than you think!

MY NAME IS: GREENLAND

What if our maps were correct?

If map apps on phones can tell us where we are almost anywhere on Earth, surely our maps ARE correct? Well, yes... maps that use satellites to guide us are pretty reliable. But the flat world maps that you'll see on the wall in lots of schools are a different story. They get some things VERY wrong!

Round to flat

What shape is Earth? Yes, it's a sphere. So it's tricky to show all the countries on a single flat, rectangular map. To do it, the standard "Mercator" world map makes countries near the equator smaller than they actually are. It also makes countries near the North and South poles bigger.

Sizing up

On a Mercator map, Greenland, which is up near the North Pole, is about the same size as the entire continent of Africa. In reality, Africa is about 14 TIMES bigger! In fact, Africa is bigger than the United States, China, and Canada put together.

The first Mercator world map was made by Flemish mapmaker Gerardus Mercator, in 1569.

I'm bigger than you think!

MY NAME IS: AFRICA

Different world

The "Gall-Peters" map is a flat map that tries to get closer to showing the true size of the world's countries. Have a look at how small Europe is next to Africa – and how much bigger South America is! With this map, though, the exact shapes of the countries are wrong. It's impossible to show the correct sizes AND shapes of countries on a flat map. That means a flat map can never be correct. You really need a sphere for that.

The answer?

It's impossible to perfectly show a sphere of countries on a flat map. But the map that we're familiar with – the Mercator map – is a bad guide to how big they all are. In fact, when it comes to size, it's often wrong! If our maps were all correct, they'd always be globes.

What if we couldn't see the stars at night?

We can't see the stars during the day because light from the Sun outshines them. But imagine going outside at night, looking up – and not seeing A SINGLE star. The sky would certainly be a less sparkly place. But human history would be different, too...

Our closest star, the Sun, is 150 million km (93 million miles) away.

North and south

You can work out how far north or south you are on Earth with just two things. One: a map of the stars, and two: a gadget called an astrolabe (said A-stroh-layb) that lets you measure the angles between the stars and the horizon. This method was popular for hundreds of years. Imagine having to rely on it now!

Stars might LOOK like diamonds in the sky, but they're actually massive, glowing balls of super-hot gas!

Useful stars

In the northern hemisphere, the bright North Star (also called Polaris) sits above the North Pole. If you're looking at it, you know you're facing north. In the southern hemisphere, the star at the "foot" of the Southern Cross always points towards the South Pole. These stars can be used to help navigate during the night.

Star signs

To make it easier to learn the positions of the stars, people divided the brightest ones into little groups or "constellations". One system which developed in western Asia more than 2,000 years ago is the zodiac. This includes 12 constellations that circle the sky. Today, these constellations are known as Aries, Taurus, Gemini, Cancer, Leo, Virgo, Libra, Scorpio, Sagittarius, Capricorn, Aquarius, and Pisces. In other parts of the world, people divided the stars up differently. Some constellations can only be seen from either the northern or the southern hemisphere, while others are visible in both.

MISSING

Cancer   Libra   Leo

The answer?

In some places it can be hard to see the stars because of light pollution (or when clouds are in the way). But if we could NEVER see the stars at night, it would have been a LOT harder for our ancestors to find their way around the planet on long voyages. And the night sky would be a lot duller to look at.

Glossary

acid substance that can react with other things and damage them. Strong acid can cause burns

asteroid chunk of rock that orbits the Sun. Asteroids are much smaller than planets or moons

atmosphere layer of gases around a planet. Earth's weather happens in the lowest parts of its atmosphere

biome large area with a similar climate and the plants and animals adapted to that climate, such as hot desert, rainforest, and tropical grassland

carbon dioxide gas that people and animals breathe out. It is also released when fossil fuels are burned

climate usual weather in a place over many years. Temperature, rainfall, and wind all affect the climate

comet large ball of ice and dust that orbits the Sun. When they pass close to the Sun, comets develop long tails

continent very large area of land and its surrounding islands. There are seven continents: Africa, Antarctica, Asia, Europe, North America, Oceania, and South America

core centre of a planet. Earth's core is very hot and made of metal

crust outer layer of a planet. Earth's crust includes land, mountains, and the ocean floor

DNA code inside the cells of every living thing that tells its body how to grow and work

extinct when an animal or plant no longer exists anywhere on Earth

fossil fuel fuel such as coal, oil, and natural gas that is made from dead plants and animals that were buried underground for millions of years

glacier very slow-moving river of ice. Glaciers form in Earth's coldest places and can shape the land over time

greenhouse gas gas, such as carbon dioxide, that traps heat in the atmosphere. Greenhouse gases can change the climate of a planet

ice sheet huge layer of ice that covers a part of Earth for a long time. Antarctica has the largest ice sheet on Earth

lava hot, molten rock that has come out of a volcano. When lava cools, it becomes solid rock

magma hot, molten rock in Earth's crust or mantle. Active volcanoes have pockets of magma beneath them

magnetic field area around a magnet where it creates a magnetic force. Earth's magnetic field protects us from harmful space rays

mantle layer of a planet underneath the crust. Earth's mantle is very thick and made of hot, putty-like rock

mineral solid, natural substance, such as table salt, quartz, or corundum, found in rocks or on their own

moon large, natural object that orbits a planet. Moons are sometimes called "natural satellites"

North Pole topmost point on Earth, found in the Arctic. The "magnetic north pole" is not always in the same spot as the "geographic north pole"

northern hemisphere top half of the Earth, above the equator

oxygen gas in the air that people and animals need to breathe in to stay alive

planet massive, round-ish object that moves around a star. The Sun is the star that Earth moves around

recycling turning waste into something new instead of throwing it away. Recycling helps to protect the environment

sea level height of the surface of the sea. It is used to measure how tall land or buildings are

South Pole bottommost point on Earth, found in Antarctica. The "magnetic south pole" is not always in the same spot as the "geographic south pole"

southern hemisphere bottom half of the Earth, below the equator

star giant ball of hot gas in space. The Sun is our closest star and gives us heat and light

tectonic plate huge chunk of Earth's upper rocky layers that slowly moves. The movement of tectonic plates can cause earthquakes and volcanoes, and create mountain ranges

tsunami giant wave caused by an earthquake or volcanic eruption

Index

AB
algae 51, 52
Alps 24-25
Amazon Rainforest 49, 60-61
Amazon River 48-49
Andes Mountains 25, 48, 49
anglerfish 51
animals
    Amazon 48, 49
    decomposition 58, 59
    extinct 62-63
    marine 4, 5, 50-51
    rainforest and desert 60-61
asteroids 6, 7
astrolabes 68
atmosphere 6, 7, 8, 13, 33, 37, 40-41
atmospheric pressure 33
bacteria 58
biomes 61

C
camels 61
carbon 31, 57, 58
carbon dioxide 13, 55, 58
cells 56, 58, 63
climate 9, 11, 12-13, 16, 55, 61
clouds 33, 36-37, 39, 45, 55
coal 13, 31, 57, 59
compasses 18-19
constellations 69
continents 20-21
core, Earth's 14-15, 18, 56
crust, Earth's 15, 26, 27, 51

D
dawn 9, 41, 43
day and night 9
de-extinction 62-63
deserts 60-61
diamonds 31
dinosaurs 7, 20, 21, 63
DNA 7, 63
dusk 9, 41, 43

E
Earth
    composition of 14-15, 26-27
    rotation of 8-9
earthquakes 4, 5, 22-23, 27
electricity 44, 45
energy 16-17, 59
evaporation 37
extinctions 62-63

FG
forest bathing 55
fossil fuels 58, 59
fusion 17
Gall-Peters map 67
gemstones 30-31
glaciers 12, 13, 52
Great Pacific Garbage Patch 65

HI
hemispheres 10-11, 69
hot spots 27
humidity 33
hurricanes 35
hydrogen 17
hydrothermal vents 5
ice 52-53
ice ages 12-13
ice cores 13
ice sheets 53
icebergs 52, 53
igneous rocks 29
iron 15, 18, 56-57

L
latitude 11
life, origins of 7
light waves 40, 41, 42-43
lightning 44-45
longitude 11

M
magma 26, 27
magnetism 18-19
mammoths 63
mantle, Earth's 15, 27
maps 66-67
Mariana Trench 50
Mars 6, 56
Mercator map 66, 67
metals 14-15, 56-57
metamorphic rocks 29
meteorites 6-7
minerals 28, 30, 31
Moon 6, 15, 41, 43, 47
moonbows 43
mountains 24-25

NOP
navigation 69
North Star (Polaris) 69
oceans 4-5, 8, 46-47, 50-51, 64, 65
oxygen 41, 55, 56, 57
Pangaea 20
plastic 64-65
polar regions 10, 12, 18-19, 69
pollution 64, 65
polystyrene 14-15
pumice 29

R
rainbows 42-43
rainforests 49, 60-61
recycling 64, 65
rivers 48-49
rocks 28-29
rotting 58-59
rubies 30-31

S
Sahara Desert 60-61
salt 4-5
satellites 19, 66
sea levels 53
seas 50
seasons 10-11
sedimentary rocks 29
sky, colour of 40-41
soil 55, 58, 64
Southern Cross 69
space rocks 6-7
stars 5, 7, 10, 16, 17, 68-69
steel 56, 57
storms 35, 39, 44-45, 46
Sun 8, 9, 10, 16-17, 37, 40, 41, 42, 43, 68
surfing 46, 47

T
tectonic plates 20-21, 23, 25
temperature 32, 33
thunder 45
tides 47
tornadoes 38-39
trees 54-55

VW
volcanoes 4, 5, 24, 26-27
water cycle 37
water power 25
water vapour 36, 37
waterspouts 38
waves 46-47
weather forecasts 32-33
wind 33, 34-35, 38-39, 46

ACKNOWLEDGEMENTS

 **Penguin Random House**

Written by Emma Young
Illustrated by Super Freak

Senior editor Olivia Stanford
Project art editor Sonny Flynn
Designers Holly Green, Lucy Sims
Editorial assistant Anna Bonnerjea
Jacket coordinator Elin Woosnam
Managing art editor Diane Peyton Jones
Production editor Gillian Reid
Production controller Jack Matts
Associate publisher Gemma Farr
Art director Mabel Chan

Consultant Anthea Lacchia

First published in Great Britain in 2025 by
Dorling Kindersley Limited
20 Vauxhall Bridge Road,
London SW1V 2SA

The authorised representative in the EEA is
Dorling Kindersley Verlag GmbH. Arnulfstr. 124,
80636 Munich, Germany

Text copyright © Emma Young, 2025
Emma Young has asserted her right to be identified as
the author of this work
Artwork copyright © Dan Whitehouse, 2025
Copyright © 2025 Dorling Kindersley Limited
A Penguin Random House Company
10 9 8 7 6 5 4 3 2 1
004–348781–Nov/2025

All rights reserved.
No part of this publication may be reproduced,
stored in or introduced into a retrieval system,
or transmitted, in any form, or by any means (electronic,
mechanical, photocopying, recording, or otherwise),
without the prior written permission of
the copyright owner.
No part of this publication may be used or reproduced
in any manner for the purpose of training artificial
intelligence technologies or systems. In accordance
with Article 4(3) of the DSM Directive 2019/790, DK
expressly reserves this work from the text
and data mining exception.

A CIP catalogue record for this book
is available from the British Library.
ISBN: 978-0-2417-3334-9

Printed and bound in the UK

www.dk.com

MIX Paper | Supporting responsible forestry
FSC™ C018179

This book was made with Forest Stewardship Council™ certified paper – one small step in DK's commitment to a sustainable future. Learn more at www.dk.com/uk/information/sustainability

For Minnie-Bee and Berni – Emma

DK would like to thank the following people for their assistance in the preparation of this book: Lois Ware for proofreading and Helen Peters for the index.

The publisher would like to thank the following for their kind permission to reproduce their photographs:
(Key: a-above; b-below/bottom; c-centre; f-far; l-left; r-right; t-top)

5 Getty Images / iStock: Coffeekai (tr). **6 Alamy Stock Photo:** NASA Photo (bl). **6-7 Alamy Stock Photo:** Susan E. Degginger (c). **8 Alamy Stock Photo:** Peter Szekely (cl). **10-11 123RF.com:** Leonello Calvetti (tc). **10 Alamy Stock Photo:** Mikko Karjalainen (bl). **11 Alamy Stock Photo:** Mediacolor's (br). **12 Alamy Stock Photo:** Dominic Byrne (bl); James Kilgo (tl). **13 Science Photo Library:** Mikkel Juul Jensen (tl). **14 Dreamstime.com:** Georgy Dzyura (cl); Tamara Kulikova (cr). **14-15 Shutterstock.com:** Irina Iankina (Stars). **15 Alamy Stock Photo:** Emre Akkoyun (c); Irina Dmitrienko (bl). Dreamstime.com: Oksana Ermak (tc). **17 Alamy Stock Photo:** Panther Media GmbH / RobertSchneider (tr). **18 Alamy Stock Photo:** All Canada Photos / Wayne Lynch (bl). **20 Science Photo Library:** Christian Darkin (bl). **22 Alamy Stock Photo:** Nigel Spiers (tr). **24 Alamy Stock Photo:** robertharding / Roberto Moiola (tl). **Shutterstock.com:** Ganjalex (bl). **24-25 Shutterstock.com:** Ganjalex (bc). **25 Alamy Stock Photo:** Incamerastock / ICP (tc). **26 Dreamstime.com:** Alberto Masnovo (cb). **26-27 Getty Images / iStock:** Thorir Ingvarsson. **27 Science Photo Library:** Planetary Visions Ltd (tr). **28 Alamy Stock Photo:** Phil Degginger (tr). **29 Alamy Stock Photo:** Dorling Kindersley Ltd / Oxford University Museum of Natural History / Gary Ombler (bl). **Dreamstime.com:** Vvoevale (tr). **30 Dreamstime.com:** Vvoevale (bc). **Science Photo Library:** Natural History Museum, London (cl). **31 Alamy Stock Photo:** Ikonacolor (ca); Pillyphotos (ftr). **Science Photo Library:** (fcra); Francesco Zerilli / Zerillimedia (tc, tr); Science Stock Photography (cra). **32 Alamy Stock Photo:** Farlap (tl). **33 Alamy Stock Photo:** Alexander Wrigley (tc). **34 Alamy Stock Photo:** FC_Italy (bl). **35 Alamy Stock Photo:** Ben Langdon (tr). **36 Alamy Stock Photo:** Ken Welsh (br). **37 Alamy Stock Photo:** Stefano Politi Markovina (bl). **38 123RF.com:** Eric Isselee / Isselee (cla). **Alamy Stock Photo:** Luca Pescucci (br). **39 Alamy Stock Photo:** RGB Ventures / SuperStock / Jim Reed (cr). **40 Alamy Stock Photo:** Blickwinkel / P. Frischknecht (tl). **41 Dreamstime.com:** Vlad Georgescu (bl). **42 Alamy Stock Photo:** Laszlo Podor (bl). **43 Dreamstime.com:** Faithiecannoise (bl); Wirestock (tr). **44 Alamy Stock Photo:** Mauritius Images GmbH / Jonas Piontek (bl). **Shutterstock.com:** Pixus (c). **44-45 Getty Images / iStock:** Patchakorn Phom-in (Lightning); Victollio (c). **45 Getty Images:** Moment / by Mike Lyvers (tl). **46 Dreamstime.com:** Typhoonski (bl). **47 Alamy Stock Photo:** Brian Kushner (tr). **48 Alamy Stock Photo:** Mark Fox (bl); Leonid Serebrennikov (c); Magdalena Paluchowska (crb). **49 Alamy Stock Photo:** Benny Marty (bl); Robertharding / Michael DeFreitas (tr). **50 Alamy Stock Photo:** Bill Truran (clb). **50-51 Alamy Stock Photo:** Bill Truran (bc). **51 Science Photo Library:** Dante Fenolio (cr). **52 Alamy Stock Photo:** Robertharding / Michael Nolan (tr). **Dreamstime.com:** Karandaev (bc). **53 Science Photo Library:** NASA / Goddard Space Flight Center Scientific Visualization Studio (tl). **54 Dreamstime.com:** Beijada (bc). **55 Alamy Stock Photo:** Tony Tallec (tl). **56 Alamy Stock Photo:** Justin Kase z05z (tl). **57 Science Photo Library:** (tl). **58 Alamy Stock Photo:** F-Stop 1 (bl); PCJones (tl). **59 Dreamstime.com:** Threeart (tr). **60 Alamy Stock Photo:** Aleksei Glustsenko (tl). **61 Alamy Stock Photo:** Jeremy Pembrey (tr). **62 Alamy Stock Photo:** Paralaxis (cl). **64 Alamy Stock Photo:** Anjo Kan (bl); Graham Turner (cl). **Dreamstime.com:** Boris Shevchuk (tr). **65 Alamy Stock Photo:** Andrey Elkin (c); Graham Turner (br). **66 Dreamstime.com:** Roywylam (bl). **Science Photo Library:** Planetobserver (cr). **68 Dorling Kindersley:** Whipple Museum of the History of Science, Cambridge / Gary Ombler (cl). **69 Alamy Stock Photo:** Brian Donovan (tr)